These prayers, selected and arranged by the person who knew Oswald Chambers best, his wife Biddy, provide a unique glimpse into the spiritual heartbeat of a remarkable man. In them, we hear petitions for direction, pleading for a special touch from God, req with his ministry, and pure, joyou understandings of Scripture.

The prayers from January throug reflect Chambers' years as principa Training College, London (1911–1 September prayers reveal Oswald's God's guidance early in 1915. The p November and December reflect th years of his life, in which he served a chaplain to British Commonwealth Egypt during World War I (1915–1

May these prayers serve to deepen your relationship with God as you m your own.

Knocking at God's Door: The Personal Prayers of Oswald Chambers

Discovery House is affiliated with Our Daily Bread Ministries, Grand Rapids, Michigan.

Requests for permission to quote from this book should be directed to: Permissions Department, Discovery House Publishers, P.O. Box 3566, Grand Rapids, MI 49501, or contact us by e-mail at permissionsdept@dhp.org.

All Scripture quotations, unless otherwise indicated, are from the New King James Version®. Copyright © 1982 by Thomas Nelson. Used by permission. All rights reserved.

Scripture quotations marked KJV are from the King James Version of the Bible.

Scripture quotations marked NASB are from the New American Standard Bible®, copyright © 1960, 1962, 1963, 1968, 1971, 1972, 1973, 1975, 1977, 1995 by The Lockman Foundation. Used by permission. (www.Lockman.org)

ISBN: 978-1-62707-331-8

Printed in China

First printing in 2015

JANUARY 1

—⁂—

O Lord, I praise you for the revelation of your supreme Fatherhood that dawns on me through the grace of the Lord Jesus. Oh, that I may be the child of my Father in heaven!

DECEMBER 31

—⟋⟍—

Lord, in this land of brooding
silences, of great generating winds,
and fiercely-killing sun, I seem to be
brooded over by you—and what will
be the result? Keep me watching and
waiting at your doorstep.

JANUARY 2

———✦———

O Lord, enchain me to yourself with
great bonds of adoring love; encircle me
with your providence for your purposes;
enlarge me until I am more and more
capable of being of use to you.

DECEMBER 30

—⁂—

It is time, O my God, for a touch from you, one of those great transfiguring touches in which you stand out plainly and clearly from all else, brilliant moments in which I see you and worship and wonder.

JANUARY 3

——ം——

"The Lord God Omnipotent reigns!"
(Revelation 19:6). Lord, the very sound
of that phrase is great and inspiring.
May I be full of the calm peace which
comes from knowing you reign.

DECEMBER 29

—◦≋◦—

"After these things the word of the
LORD came . . . saying, 'Do not be afraid
. . . I am your shield, your exceedingly
great reward" (Genesis 15:1). O Lord,
"after these things"! How I praise you.

JANUARY 4

—✴—

Lord, how easily the mind
wanders when your domination
is not in the ascendant!
Keep the lordship of body and
soul and spirit in your hands.

DECEMBER 28

—⁓—

O Lord, this is your day, and I
implore you to bless me with
your exceeding great blessing and
benediction. How wonderful it is
to be able to approach you!

JANUARY 5

———— ✺ ————

O Lord, grant that in sweet and
gracious likeness to yourself I
might delight your heart this day,
perfect my own life, and be a pure
blessing to all around me.

DECEMBER 27

—✳—

Lord, fill every space around us with yourself this day. Control everything marvelously by your guiding hand. Lift us up into your wonderful purposes, and keep us from impulsive hastiness.

JANUARY 6

—⁂—

What a joyous life the life "hidden with
Christ in God" (Colossians 3:3) is!
But, my God, I dare not for one moment
think how far short of it I fall in spite
of all your grace and patience. But you
are making me, and I thank you.

DECEMBER 26

—◦◦◦—

O Lord, my Lord and Master, may
I be so consciously yours today
that I am at home with you, and
joyous in my childlike delight in
your possession of me.

JANUARY 7

─◆─

"And you yourselves be like men who wait for their master" (Luke 12:36)— might I be like that, waiting, eager, dutiful, alert, and full of power and presence of mind.

DECEMBER 25

—⁂—

Lord Jesus, centuries ago you were here on this earth, "manifested in the flesh" (1 Timothy 3:16). Be here again today, manifested in my flesh—"Christ in you, the hope of glory" (Colossians 1:27).

JANUARY 8

—⁓—

Lord, I look to you. How I know
that "in me nothing good dwells"
(Romans 7:18). How marvelous is
your grace that I now find in my heart
no motive save for your glory.

DECEMBER 24

—◦—

Lord, the word that strikes me so
intimately in my reading this morning
is this—"Thus did Moses; just as the
Lord had commanded him, so he did"
(Numbers 17:11).

JANUARY 9

—⟋⟍—

Lord, bring the sweetness and
fullness of your power to bear
on me this day. Oh, for the big,
the generous, the gracious, the
grave-glad life of God!

DECEMBER 23

———✦———

Lord Jesus, in you dwells "all the fullness" of God. "All things" have been delivered to you (Colossians 1:19). "All power" is given unto you in heaven and in earth (Matthew 28:18). O God, my heavenly Father, supply my every need according to your riches in glory in Christ Jesus (Philippians 4:19).

JANUARY 10

———

Send forth your light, O Lord, brood over
us as you did over chaos (Genesis 1:2).
Work mightily in your spiritual domains,
and help me to erect mountain peaks of
prayer that the clouds may be rent and
bring themselves down in blessing.

DECEMBER 22

—⁂—

O Lord, I thank you for the verse this morning—"So you, by the help of your God, return; observe mercy and justice, and wait on your God continually" (Hosea 12:6). Fill all this vast encampment with your glorious presence; restrain, and inspire godliness.

JANUARY 11

—✦—

Lord, the hilarious simplicity of trust in you seems almost levity until I remember you, and dare not *not* be glad! Spread joy and gladness all around us this day.

DECEMBER 21

—◦—

Lord, be such a reviving and refreshing presence in our midst today that we can only rejoice as fresh hopes of eternity, even in the present moment, open before our eyes.

JANUARY 12

—⚬—

Lord, this day is peculiarly
your day; help us to remember
only you. Bless your servants
all over the world.

DECEMBER 20

—∿∿—

Speak, Lord, that I may hear and understand. There seems so much external activity in my spiritual life, so little gracious power realized. Energize me until I am incandescent with you.

JANUARY 13

—◦◦◦—

O Lord, how excellent it is to
commune with you in the early
morning hours. Enable me by patience
to reproduce these exalted moments of
calm into the activities of the day.

DECEMBER 19

———— ·§· ————

Lord, this one thing—my utterable
and unutterable need of you. "Poor in
spirit" (Matthew 5:3) describes my
certain knowledge of myself. In entire
necessity I come to you.

JANUARY 14

———∿∿∿———

"Oft shall that flesh imperil and outweary"—
yet what indignation does this bear in me!
As I rouse myself, meet my rousing with the
inspiration of your Spirit.

————

Today's prayer opens with a line from the poem
"Saint Paul" by Frederic William Henry Myers.

DECEMBER 18

—∞—

"Great is our Lord, and mighty in power; His understanding is infinite" (Psalm 147:5). How certainly all might and wisdom is yours, and how certainly by your grace I am eager for you to have your way through me.

JANUARY 15

Lord, lift up the light of your countenance upon me and give me peace, your peace, deep as the unfathomed sea, high as the unscaled heights of heaven. Touch me now, till light and life and liberty course through me.

DECEMBER 17

—⁓—

Lord, my approach to you
is dulled because of physical
dimness, but my heart is glad, and
my body also shall rest in hope.

JANUARY 16

—⚬—

Lord, I would worship you in the
psalmist's words—"Unto the upright
there arises light in the darkness" (112:4).
O Lord, how supreme a darkness I am!
Therefore you must be the light.

DECEMBER 16

—⁓—

Lord, how eager is my growing
desire for you, not in any small,
narrow manner, but in the glorious
manner of a fuller realization of
your holiness.

JANUARY 17

——— ❦ ———

Lord, I come to you in helplessness,
yet in hopefulness in-wrought by your
Spirit, that I might be filled with
your love, your divine selfless nature,
your passionate patience, unwounded
by personal considerations.

DECEMBER 15

—◦—

Lord, I turn implicitly to you.
Be such an atmosphere in and
around us that we may be those
out of whom the rivers of living
water flow (John 7:38).

JANUARY 18

—◆◆◆—

O Lord, this day put your touch,
great and ennobling and inspiring,
upon us all. Save completely our
minds from panic and our spirits
from undue haste.

DECEMBER 14

—◦◦◦—

Lord, I look to you. Touch my body till it is all radiant with your life. Bless the morning service and make it glorious with your presence.

JANUARY 19

———ᗢᗢᗢ———

Lord, how I realize the peril of work
and activity equally with that of quiet
and seclusion, and that the only secure
haven is yourself. Help me to be taken
up completely with you.

DECEMBER 13

—⁂—

Lord, to you I turn, and on the ground of your mighty redemption I pray great triumphing prayers with "the confidence that we have in Him, that if we ask anything according to His will, He hears us" (1 John 5:14).

JANUARY 20

—⚬—

O Lord, I look to you so utterly
that I am worse than useless
without you. Be wisdom and
discernment and understanding
to me today.

DECEMBER 12

—⁂—

Lord, I praise you for this sense
of joyful fellowship with you again.
Give me calmness of mind and
keenness of purpose. Keep me yours,
undoubtedly and without deflection.

JANUARY 21

—⚶—

O Lord, this day keep us so well
that we never need to think
of ourselves at all, but joyously
spend and be spent for you.

DECEMBER 11

—✦—

"Now therefore, O God, strengthen my hands" (Nehemiah 6:9)—Lord, now! Come to me, fill me with yourself, then there will be no yearning unsatisfied.

JANUARY 22

—◦—

O Lord, if I am strong in any way it is only in you. This morning my soul rejoices because I recall the word "Be strong in the Lord and in the power of His might" (Ephesians 6:10).

DECEMBER 10

—◦◦◦—

Lord, in my consciousness this morning
a crowd of little things press and I bring
them straight to your presence. In your
wisdom, say, "Peace, be still!" (Mark 4:39)
and may our ordered lives confess the
beauty of your peace.

JANUARY 23

— ⁓ —

O Lord, in simple dependence on
your Holy Spirit indwelling in me
and uniting me with your nature,
I look to you; cause me to be all you
would have me be.

DECEMBER 9

—⁂—

Lord, I rejoice that with you, the Father of lights, there can be "no variation or shadow of turning" (James 1:17). Help me to discern your rule and authority.

JANUARY 24

—✦—

O Lord, lift up the light of your
countenance upon us, let your great
and glorious voice and presence
sweep through this college. On those
of us who teach send the Spirit and
gracious insight into your truth.

DECEMBER 8

—◦◦◦—

Lord, sustain all who are taxed physically. Prevent the exacting of the enemy, and may the joy of the Lord be their strength in a marvelous manner.

JANUARY 25

Lord, how dim and distant
and dreary my physical life
seems, and is, without you.
Fill me with your divine life.

DECEMBER 7

———✦———

I praise you, O Lord, for the word this
morning—"Now when Moses went into
the tabernacle of meeting to speak with
Him, he heard the voice of One speaking
to him from above the mercy seat; . . . thus
He spoke to him" (Numbers 7:89).

JANUARY 26

—⁓—

O Lord, as this your day unfolds be
our special treasure in everything
(Exodus 19:5). Permeate us with your
Spirit that all may be transfigured with
sweet contented spiritual power.

DECEMBER 6

—∾—

O Lord, explore down to
the deepest springs of my
spirit where the Spirit makes
intercession for us, and read
the prayers I cannot utter.

JANUARY 27

—∽—

O Lord, I come to you; consciously and
unconsciously, I draw near in uttermost
need. Lift me, lead me, fill me for your
glory, make me harmoniously one with
your purpose and will.

DECEMBER 5

—⁂—

Lord, not with any sense of
unworthiness (how can unworthiness
indulge in any sense of worthiness?),
not any thought of my insufficiency,
nor any thought of myself at all, I come
just because you are yourself.

JANUARY 28

—∞—

O God, increase my sense of you
and my understanding of your Son,
my Lord and Master. Grant that I
may more and more realize your
dominance and rule, and more and
more rejoice in simple joy in you.

DECEMBER 4

———— ∞ ————

Lord, to you I come. Entrench me around with yourself as a wall of fire and be the glory in the midst. This sounds entirely selfish, but I do not know how else to put it. O Lord, you know.

JANUARY 29

—⁂—

O Lord, you are ever well, and all my
fresh springs are in you (Psalm 87:7).
I come to you; may your mighty life
spring up in me, a veritable influx into
body as well as spirit.

DECEMBER 3

———∞———

How often I find it is the stubborn donkey in me rather than my intelligence that turns aside and sees the angel of the Lord (Numbers 22:23). Lord, increase my spiritual sensitiveness that I may detect your slightest goings and drawings.

JANUARY 30

———

Lord, today let your praise abound, let
joy and gladness resound everywhere.
How I long for joy—great, bounding,
liberating joy: joy in God, joy in the Holy
Spirit, joy in life, and joy in love. Cause
this to be a joyous house today, all day.

DECEMBER 2

O Lord, cause this "rod" to bud. Make the study classes flourish before you, even as "the rod of Aaron ... had sprouted and put forth buds, had produced blossoms" (Numbers 17:8).

JANUARY 31

⚬⚬⚬

Lord, your ways are like yourself—
perfect. My ways are like myself—
imperfect. Touch me into an effective,
working identity with your mind and
with your ways for this day.

DECEMBER 1

⁓

Lord, how dense and foggy it still
is on my spiritual, or rather my
mental horizon, so that details take
threatening dimensions and crowd
out the great issues of life. Liberate
me with your deliverance.

FEBRUARY 1

—⁓—

Lord God Almighty, you are holy; but more wonderful than praise can tell, you undertake to make me holy by your grace.

NOVEMBER 30

———————

Lord, to you I come, absolutely come.
I feel so entire a sense of need of you
that I just wait for you to speak to
me, for what can I say to you? Let me
lie spread out before you even as the
desert sand beneath the sun.

FEBRUARY 2

—~~~—

O Lord, how little I realize what it means
to watch with you, to continue with you
in your temptations (Matthew 26:36–46).
Draw me nearer this morning and insulate
me by your mighty power until I speak
and live only for you.

NOVEMBER 29

———⟨⟩———

Lord, give me a fresh anointing of your Spirit for today, in prayer, in worship, and in work, so that in all things you might have the preeminence.

FEBRUARY 3

Lord, breathe on me until my frame is knit to your thought. Lift me until I see your face and trust your almightiness without fear or insidious unbelief.

NOVEMBER 28

—~⚬~—

Lord, I thank you for the touch you have given me this morning—but what amazing lethargy has been mine, what un-beautifulness! Yet this is only a revelation of what I know myself to be apart from your life in me.

FEBRUARY 4

—◦◦◦—

Lord, I praise you for your word—
"By your patience possess your souls"
(Luke 21:19), and I praise you for
your grace which waits while I
laboriously acquire the soul you
would have me acquire.

NOVEMBER 27

—◦—

Lord, I am conscious of a lack
of proportion—things that are
the merest trifles loom, and the
glorious things recede. Give me a
way out that I may be to your glory.

FEBRUARY 5

—⁂—

O Lord, to you I turn, to you.
I am but a homeless waif until
you touch me with the security
of your peace, the sweet sense
of your love.

NOVEMBER 26

—⁓—

O Lord, to you I come for this day.
The degenerating tendencies of
this place are subtle to a degree of
amazement! Restore the joy of life
which makes all around radiant.

FEBRUARY 6

—∾—

Lord, your word comes so quietly and all-pervadingly—"If anyone serves Me, let him follow Me" and "If anyone serves Me, him My Father will honor" (John 12:26). Take me as your servant in this sense.

NOVEMBER 25

—◦◦◦—

"Thy touch has still its ancient power."
Touch me, Lord, into fellowship with
yourself till my whole being glows with
your peace and joy.

———

Quotation from the hymn "At Even, Ere the
Sun Was Set" by Henry Twells.

FEBRUARY 7

———

O Lord, how wholesome and grand a
thing it is to be willing toward you.
I am willing, eagerly willing for your
will to be done, and I feel all deeply
joyful at the prospect, for nothing can
be so glorious as just your will.

NOVEMBER 24

—※—

O Lord, I fully realize that "I am a
little child; I do not know how to
go out or come in" (1 Kings 3:7).
Give me therefore "an understanding
heart" (verse 9), and increase my
sense of you this day.

FEBRUARY 8

—⚬—

How I long to be so full of
you, burning and shining and
irradiating you, that there is no
room for anything but just your
gracious light.

NOVEMBER 23

———

Lord, how little nourishment I have been giving to the indwelling Christ in me. O Lord, forgive me. Fill me with the ample sense of your forgiveness that I may not only joy in your salvation, but be filled with your Spirit for the work here.

FEBRUARY 9

—⁓—

O Lord, speak with power and
graciousness in today's services.
Conduct me into the secret of
fellowship with you that you may
be able to convey yourself perfectly.

NOVEMBER 22

———— ·◊· ————

Lord, this day give me the most
supreme absorption in you—such
distractions, such drainings! I would
return home to you, living again the
life of entire dependence on you.

FEBRUARY 10

—⚬—

O Lord, in some moods it seems so easy to slip
away from you and your purposes. And yet,
Lord, I do not believe it is. But I do believe it is
possible to enter into your purposes like a beast
of the field, with no discernment and no vision.
Lord, I would be a son of yours.

NOVEMBER 21

—◦◦◦—

"Let me hear your voice" (Song of
Solomon 2:14)—that is my prayer.
I am willing beyond all my expression
to hear you, to perceive you, to be
thrilled with your presence.

FEBRUARY 11

—✦—

O Lord, how I need infilling and
invigorating by your presence.
Give me that buoyant, quiet
confidence in you which is the
witness of the Spirit.

NOVEMBER 20

———⋙———

Lord, today give me the intuitive,
instinctive inspiration of your Holy
Spirit that I may discern you in all
things. Fill the whole day with your
gracious presence and peace.

FEBRUARY 12

—⁂—

O Lord, my soul praises you for its trust in you. My soul hangs on your touch and smile lest any distraction of mind or imagination arise and I be corrupted from the simplicity that is in Christ.

NOVEMBER 19

~m~

Lord, I thank you for the counsel in the text this morning—"And let it be . . . that you do as the occasion demands; for God is with you" (1 Samuel 10:7)—not to fret myself into conscious usefulness, but just do as the occasion you have engineered shall serve.

FEBRUARY 13

———≈———

O Lord, I would crave more
and more to put on love like a
garment, that in my contact with
people that is what they will most
lastingly recognize.

NOVEMBER 18

—◦—

Lord, bless with significant blessing
the start of the study classes
tonight. Bring keenness of interest
and spiritual power to bear strongly
and mightily upon us all.

FEBRUARY 14

———❦———

O Lord, that the most absorbing
sensing of you might be mine, that
your will should be done in and
through me without hindrance.

NOVEMBER 17

———✦———

O Lord, I thank you for yesterday, and for the fleeting realization of your depths in me. Enable me this day to join heart and mind to you in steady and constant prayer.

FEBRUARY 15

—◦◦◦—

O Lord, how I adore you, but how I
long for more conscious adoration and
communion and God-praising-ness.
Cleanse me from the defilement of
distance from you.

NOVEMBER 16

---✺---

O Lord, this sense of being
choked with immediately
present things is suffocating to
our realization of yourself.
Come and deliver and delight us.

FEBRUARY 16

—⁓—

Here is the day, O Lord,
your day, cause it to shine
forever in our individual lives
like a jewel.

NOVEMBER 15

—⟫⟪—

O Lord, be so really present here
in this hut that every man coming
in may realize that it is God's
house in deed and in truth.

FEBRUARY 17

———⌇———

O Lord, I do thank you for the
condition of heart and motive your
grace has wrought in me, but, oh, when
in my actual life shall I express before
the world the beauty of your peace?

NOVEMBER 14

Lord, I seem to drift around, just living dimly before you until you spring up within me. I adore you that I have faith in your mighty redemption, but oh, it makes such a difference to realize your touch!

FEBRUARY 18

—⫘—

Guard my central life from corrosion, O Lord. Keep me secretly so right with you that my life glorifies you.

NOVEMBER 13

—⟐—

O Lord, how completely true of me is the
psalmist's word—"My soul clings to the dust"
(Psalm 119:25). My soul is very dusty, Lord.
Quicken me according to your word. One word
made living by your Spirit and how exquisite is
the life that comes! Lord, speak it now.

FEBRUARY 19

—⁓—

I praise you for that word—"As a father pities his children, so the LORD pities those who fear Him" (Psalm 103:13). How I realize that I owe nothing to your severity but all to your love. Oh, that your love and gentleness and patience toward me were expressed through me to others!

NOVEMBER 12

Lord, lift me up to you so that the bloom, the radiant joy of your salvation, visits me and shines forth for your glory. Keep me in flowing intercession with you.

FEBRUARY 20

———❧———

O Lord, one thing amazes me, and that
is my almost total deficiency in letting
you manifest yourself and your beauty
in my outward life. Let the beauty of
the Lord our God be upon me this day.

NOVEMBER 11

—⁓—

Lord, bless this day with great evidence of your thoughts toward us. I praise you for your word this morning—"For I know the thoughts that I think toward you, says the LORD, thoughts of peace and not of evil" (Jeremiah 29:11).

FEBRUARY 21

—◦◦◦—

O Lord, with much dimness
I draw near to you. Clear the
dimness away from me and
flood me with the light of
your countenance.

NOVEMBER 10

—✳—

Lord, cause this day to be filled with your praise. Give me release from this medley of distractions, from attentiveness of nerves to all the details that press. I praise you that my mind *is* stayed on you, but I do desire your beauty to be upon me.

FEBRUARY 22

———⁓———

O Lord, I beg you for sustaining
strength and simple joy. Keep me
humble-minded in motive and design
that nothing of the self-satisfied,
superior person may be mine.

NOVEMBER 9

———

O Lord, fill our bodies, this encampment, the whole Earth, with your glorious self this day. Bless with flooding tides of spiritual life all of us today, just for the delight of it!

FEBRUARY 23

—⁓—

O Lord, how much of a lift I need
this morning! You know. In my
preaching, cause your glorious voice
to be heard, your lovely face to be seen,
your pervasive Spirit felt.

NOVEMBER 8

———✦———

Lord, be manifest in our midst
today, give us the great objective
certainty of your presence. This
bungalow, make it Bethany indeed,
a house beautiful with God.

FEBRUARY 24

—⚬—

Cleanse me, O Lord, from all
complicity of spirit, and
may your radiant beauty be
in and upon me this day.

NOVEMBER 7

—✺—

Lord, quicken my sense of you, my
discernment of you, my concentration
on you, so that I am carefully careless
about every relationship except my
relationship with you.

FEBRUARY 25

—⁓—

How depressed and appalled
I am at the prospect of sinking to
the commonplace! Lord, help me
to live purely and powerfully and
fascinatedly yours.

NOVEMBER 6

———

In all matters, O Lord, I would acknowledge you. Keep us in tune with you that others may catch the joyousness and gladness of God.

FEBRUARY 26

—⚬—

Oh, for one of those touches
of your Spirit that, as the
wind, quicken and awaken,
loosen and inspire!

NOVEMBER 5

—·—

Lord, I do praise you for the inestimable
privilege of this early morning
communion with you. Work in me that
I may both will and work for your good
pleasure this day (Philippians 2:13).

FEBRUARY 27

─⊷﹏⊷─

How my heart and my flesh cry out for the living God! Oh, the exhaustion of myself! And oh, the refreshment and joy of the Lord!

NOVEMBER 4

———⚬———

Today, O Lord, cleanse me from
flurried busyness, and keep me
calmly and purely yours. Make
this hut the house of God, and the
gate of heaven to men's souls.

FEBRUARY 28

⸻

O Lord, in complete need I turn to
you. Come to me physically, mentally,
morally, and spiritually, and cause me
to bring about the manifestation of
yourself that is glorifying to you.

NOVEMBER 3

—✦—

Lord, these words come with the dawning power of your Spirit's might—"He takes away the first that He may establish the second" (Hebrews 10:9). How I praise you for every remembrance of the college—it is never far from my thoughts. That is "the first," and what will be "the second"?

FEBRUARY 29

—⁓—

Oh, how I long to be all taken up by you,
all my body, soul, and spirit energized
by you—so many lurking things of the
darkness still remain. What a gracious
humiliation these things are.

NOVEMBER 2

—✺—

O Lord, I beseech you to bring me into living union with your purpose for these [YMCA] huts I am in charge of. Anoint me afresh for this day in all its opportunity. Let me see your salvation at work.

MARCH 1

—⚬—

I praise you that all I am is yours.
Oh, that I could delight you as
the lily does, or the tree, or even
the sparrows, just living the life
you have granted!

NOVEMBER 1

—⁂—

Lord, this day be the restraining One
in the midst of these thousands
of soldiers. Many of them are
godless—you did die for "the ungodly."
Cause them to turn to you.

MARCH 2

—⁓—

O Lord God, what you are to me I
dimly begin to discern—more than
morning light, more than joy and health,
more than all your blessings. Dawn on
me afresh this morning and make me
light all through with your light.

OCTOBER 31

—⁂—

We thank you that there is
no good-bye. We ask you that
your crown and seal may be
upon us every one until we see
you face-to-face.

MARCH 3

—✦—

O Lord, my soul would wait upon you
as Creator of the world, and upon our
Lord Jesus Christ as Creator of His life
in me. Oh, for the power of your Spirit
to adore you in fuller measure!

OCTOBER 30

———✦———

Lord, what powerful words come this morning: "Be strong and of good courage; do not be afraid, nor be dismayed, for the LORD your God is with you wherever you go" (Joshua 1:9). Amen! Hallelujah!

MARCH 4

—✺—

"The tops of the pillars were in the shape of lilies" (1 Kings 7:22). O Lord, this word is in my mind, especially how devoid I am of any "lily work," so rugged and unadorned. Cause me to be yours in the expression of your grace as well as in the experience of it.

OCTOBER 29

—⁓—

Lord, to you I come. Give me a gracious inflow of your life till my reasoning, my imagination, and my speaking are all of you. How grandly you have renewed my spirit and restored to me the joy of your salvation!

MARCH 5

O Lord, this new day enable me by your grace to fully feel your nearness and your might. Keep me facing your glory that I may be "transformed into the same image from glory to glory" (2 Corinthians 3:18).

OCTOBER 28

—⚬—

Lord, I thank you for the past night's sleep. I bless you that you neither slumber nor sleep but keep us by day and by night.

MARCH 6

—ᴍ—

How manifold are the ways I need
you! I praise you that you are there
to be found. Lord, let me find you.
It is only when you come yourself
that I find you.

OCTOBER 27

---⚬⚬---

Lord, this day be God, so great,
so kind, so full of life and liberty;
come in grace and power. I praise
you for the beauty of the morning.

MARCH 7

—◦◦—

I would, O Lord, have all my
thought and emotions and words
fragrant with love, perfect love to
you, and through that to others.

OCTOBER 26

—◆◆◆—

Lord, with praise and adoration
I come to you this Sabbath
morning. I bless you for the
inspiring association of my life
and upbringing with Sunday.

MARCH 8

—m—

O my God, I lie in your fire burning
and purifying—so much dross I seem
to discover today, so little of your sweet
and lovely grace in my dealing with
others' faults. Lord, forgive me.

OCTOBER 25

—✦—

O Lord, to you I come with an overwhelming sense of spiritual dryness and deficiency. Replenish me, O Lord, for your name's sake. I will not mourn before you but be filled with your Spirit.

MARCH 9

—◆—

O Lord, soften and subdue,
inspire and thrill, and raise us
to the level of such glorious
communion with you that we
may catch your likeness.

OCTOBER 24

—⁓—

Lord, dawn on me this day, draw
me, direct me into all the beauty
of your divine purposes; touch my
senses that I may see your ways
and delight in them.

MARCH 10

—◆—

O Lord, how wonderful and
great and mighty it is to turn
toward you. Keep me from
any dominance saving yours.

OCTOBER 23

———— ❧ ————

"You must not fear them, for the LORD your God Himself fights for you" (Deuteronomy 3:22). Lord, this word came to me insistently in my reading this morning. How entirely I look to you!

MARCH 11

O Lord, tone me up with your great power. I believe I am privileged to ask this because of the atonement of Jesus. Make me physically all I ought to be so that your radiance may be on me.

OCTOBER 22

—∾∾—

O Lord, restore the unique joy of your
presence to me and make me yours and
of you in this place. I seem unsuited
for anything but just waiting on you.
Show me a token for good, O Lord.

MARCH 12

—⁓—

Lord, your face, your touch, your
blessing I seek today. Touch me,
Lord, till every part of my being
vibrates and thrills with your gracious
and powerful well-being.

OCTOBER 21

—✵—

Lord, I thank you for the word this morning—"The Lord upholds him with His hand" (Psalm 37:24). Ah Lord, and you do talk to me with the pressure of your hand.

MARCH 13

—◆—

Lord, my chief desire is to be rooted
and grounded in you—God-centered
and God-absorbed, God-enthused and
God-loved. How eager my soul is to
know you and be still!

OCTOBER 20

———❦———

Lord, what need is mine! What
weaknesses lurk in hidden places and
mar my whole being. O Lord, I turn to
you. How I need to realize that apart
from you I can do nothing.

MARCH 14

—❦—

O Lord, how wonderful are
your ways! When I recall the
way you have led me and been
patient with me, I am lost in
wonder, love, and praise.

OCTOBER 19

—⦅⦆—

O Lord, I have to preach in your name today. Shall I, must I, speak on "God is love"? Am I to do it without your mighty inspiration and thrilling power? No, Lord, forbid it.

MARCH 15

—⚬—

Bless us here today, O Lord—
so many need you. Go in and
out among us, controlling and
lifting with your saving power.

OCTOBER 18

—∞—

Lord, give me discernment and
inspiration for today's classes.
Bless this day and make it
radiant with your power.

MARCH 16

———⁓———

O Lord, what a wonder of perfect
confidence it would create could I
but hear some clear, decisive word
of yours! Lord, speak it today.

OCTOBER 17

—◊—

Lord, let me see you today fully
and freely. Keep a clear space
between you and me that I may
see the way by which I should go.

MARCH 17

—❦—

O Lord, by your grace open
my vision to you and your
infinite horizons, and take me
into your counsels regarding
your work in this college.

OCTOBER 16

---※---

Lord, I praise you that you are,
and that you perform your
perfect will in and through the
lives of individual people.

MARCH 18

O Lord, I would that I had
a livelier sense of you and of
your abundance continually
with me.

OCTOBER 15

———

Lord, cause it to be proven that
I shall be "like a tree planted by
the rivers of water" (Psalm 1:3),
bringing forth its fruit in its season.

MARCH 19

—⚬—

O Lord, bless me this hour with the glow of your presence and sense of your nearness. I do trust only in you, yet I long for conscious delight in your presence, if you will graciously grant it to me.

OCTOBER 14

—✦—

Lord, I come to you this morning
with a sense of spiritual failure.
Cleanse me by your grace, and
restore me to the heavenly places
in Christ Jesus.

MARCH 20

—◦—

O Lord, may this day be glorious
with your presence and blessing.
May we see you causing the "place
of [your] feet" (Isaiah 60:13)
to be glorious.

OCTOBER 13

———

Lord, increase my certainty that I am taken up
into your consciousness, and not that I take
you into mine. "For in all the world there is
none but thee, my God, there is none but thee."

———

Quotation from the poem "Saint Paul"
by Frederic William Henry Myers.

MARCH 21

—⁂—

O Lord, I praise you for the mighty lines of thought that come as I consider membership in your mystical body (1 Corinthians 12:12–14). How I long to be quickened enough to realize the wonder of it more.

OCTOBER 12

—⌇—

Lord, your servant's words state my deepest
prayer—"My God, I look to thee for
tenderness such as I could not seek from any
man, or in a human heart fancy or plan."

Quotation from *The Diary of an Old Soul*
by George MacDonald.

MARCH 22

——❦——

O Lord, you are my God; I know
no God beside you. My sense of
unworthiness is so great that I do not
waste any time in telling you of it.
It is to you I come—yearningly,
eagerly, completely.

OCTOBER 11

—※—

Lord, I praise you for the sense of
well-being which is mine this morning.
How I praise you for the deep
revelation of redemption! Shine with
unclouded ray upon us all.

MARCH 23

—❦—

O Lord, I pray for supplies of your grace today, grace so divine and mighty that many may glorify you through my ministry.

OCTOBER 10

—◦〰◦—

"Cleanse me from secret faults.
Keep back Your servant also from
presumptuous sins" (Psalm 19:12–13).
Oh that I could find you exhibiting in
me your peace and purity!

MARCH 24

—〰—

Lord God Almighty, who was
manifested in Jesus Christ, I
come before you now with the
unpretentiousness of a human being
needing you absolutely and rejoicing
in my need.

OCTOBER 9

—◁◈▷—

Lord, the present position presses most
on my consciousness this morning.
Cause my mind, my emotions, my
whole nature, to want what you have
ordained for me, that thereby I may
know I have done right.

MARCH 25

——⚬——

O Lord, when I awake, I am still
with you. Quicken my mortal
body with your mighty resurrection
life; rouse me this hour with a
gracious influx of power.

OCTOBER 8

—ɯɯ—

"Indeed, these are the mere edges of His ways . . . . But the thunder of His power who can understand?" (Job 26:14). So many homeless moods float through my soul. I have no wisdom, no understanding of things pertaining to you until you lighten my darkness.

MARCH 26

"Clouds and darkness surround Him; righteousness and justice are the foundation of His throne" (Psalm 97:2). Commune with me, O Lord, that I may know I am light in you.

OCTOBER 7

—⁓—

But surely, Lord, I do not need more
verification of the truth of your words
concerning the human heart. If it be your
will, I do not want to know any more along
that line. I want to know more of the great
and gracious reality of your redemption.

MARCH 27

—⁂—

O Lord, the "multitudes" will be coming and going today. Help me to keep, like my Master, in the lonely places and pray (Luke 5:15–16).

OCTOBER 6

———✦———

Lord, how wondrous is the thought of you! But when shall I find my willing heart all taken up by you? I seem to be paralyzed by my own littleness and pettiness and sinfulness.

MARCH 28

---—◦◦◦—---

O Lord, visit with your tenderness
every heart and life that has
been experiencing the shattering
which the penetration of your
word brings.

OCTOBER 5

—⁂—

Lord God Omnipotent, give me
wisdom this day to worship you
properly and be well-pleasing to you.
Interpret yourself to me more and
more in your fullness and beauty.

MARCH 29

—⁓—

O Lord, guide and determine
our steps so that our mouths
shall be filled with laughter at
what you will bring to pass!

OCTOBER 4

———✦———

Lord, I praise you for the joy of my life
here—for the love of wife and child,
for the students, for the favors of the
Holy Spirit. What a wonder of joy and
radiant blessing this place has been!

MARCH 30

—⸙—

O Lord, be very present
today—the great joyous
presence of the Holy Spirit
permeating everywhere.

OCTOBER 3

—⁂—

Lord, I have no inkling of your ways
in external details, but I have the
expectancy of your wonders soon to be
made visible. How completely at rest I
am, and how free from seeing your way.

MARCH 31

— ⚬⚬ —

O Lord, I seem an incarnate desert
before you, unbeautiful and arid;
but, praise your name, you can make
the desert "rejoice and blossom as the
rose" (Isaiah 35:1).

OCTOBER 2

⸻⸻

"When He hides His face, who then can see Him?" (Job 34:29). There is so little sign of your being with us in these days of waiting. I pray not for any sign of outward success, but I do seek the sense of your blessing and approval.

APRIL 1

—◦◦◦—

O Lord, the truth that presses its way through all else this morning is the truth about sanctification. Forgive me if I have imperceptibly shifted from this great purpose of yours.

OCTOBER 1

—⌇—

Lord, carry me into your counsels and use me for your glory. For this college, may no fever of energy obstruct your working. Correct us in measure and in tenderness till we make it easy for you to carry out your plans through us.

APRIL 2

———◦———

O Lord, blessed be the tone and power
of your voice, its tones of tenderness
and love in grace; its tones of power in
the great gales of nature. Lord, cause
your glorious voice to be heard in this
college and in my soul.

SEPTEMBER 30

———※———

Lord, when I remember all your
goodness, your wonders and your
grace, I alternate between praise and
apprehension. O Lord, my prayer is
that all you seek in me should be carried
out in daily application to my life.

APRIL 3

———— ∞ ————

Draw me, O Lord, into vital communion
with yourself. What a difference the
sun makes in the natural world—and
what a difference it makes when you
dawn upon us! Press through till we are
thrilled with your presence.

SEPTEMBER 29

———~———

Lord, touch me again in body, soul, and spirit. If my food and drink are hindering your ways in and through me, reveal this to me and keep me yours, so that whether I eat or drink, or whatsoever I do, may it be to your glory (1 Corinthians 10:31).

APRIL 4

—⁓—

O Lord, how miserly is my appreciation
of your atonement and perfect salvation.
Lord, draw me into fuller gratitude.
Let me ever be a passionate lover of the
Lord Jesus Christ.

SEPTEMBER 28

—◦◦◦—

Lord, bring me closer and
nearer to you until I am more
and more useful to you in
your enterprises.

APRIL 5

—❦—

O Lord, my Lord, make this
day glorious. For myself in
your service, I ask reprieve
from all distractions.

SEPTEMBER 27

—⁂—

Lord, this day glorify yourself.
Light up this house, my body,
with your glory so that from all
windows you might look forth
unhindered and radiant.

APRIL 6

———

O Lord, I praise you for your
mighty redemption at the heart
of all our problems. By your great
power raise us up to newness of
life this Easter Day.

SEPTEMBER 26

—⁕—

Lord, of late I feel a dim uncertainty as
if you are leading me into a domain of
truth that as yet I have not entered or
penetrated. Lord, lift me up till I see
you; hold me till I fulfill your purpose.

APRIL 7

——◆——

O Lord, the wonder of being one with
you as you are one with the Father!
Grant us this oneness for your glory,
and to that end lift up the light of your
countenance upon us and give us peace.

SEPTEMBER 25

---ⁿ⁓⁓⁓---

O Lord, for the days of this vacation I praise
and thank you—for the majesty of this
crowded isolation, the leagues of moor, the
radiant air, the tonic of naturalness, and the
sweet tonic of spiritual instruction as I lie
open to your grace.

APRIL 8

———

O Lord, cause my intellect
to glow with your Holy
Spirit's teaching.

SEPTEMBER 24

—⚬—

O Lord, I thank you for the fullness of
tone and health you give us these days.
Continue it, O Lord. Save from all
false emotion and sentimentality and
sadness, and with vigor and gladness
bless each one of us this day.

APRIL 9

—✦—

O Lord, your graciousness is fresh
to my soul, but how slow is my
growth in your almighty grace!
Energize me, open my nature to
grander horizons this day.

SEPTEMBER 23

—⁓—

Lord, I thank you for the profound
and eager joy with which I find myself
looking for your second coming!
Oh that I might find grace in your
sight, and behave more worthily of
your great salvation!

APRIL 10

―⁓―

O Lord, I praise you for the prayers of
fellow Christians which have surrounded
me like an atmosphere of heaven, and
for the unspeakable grace which comes to
me through your redemption.

SEPTEMBER 22

—◆◆◆—

O Lord, the sternness, the unrelieved
sternness, of my morning subject with
the students [Jeremiah]. Soften the
truths to our understanding, and keep
us strong in you.

APRIL 11

—∞—

Be radiant through me, O Lord.
Give me your approving smile and
benediction, and help me to be
fully taken up with you.

SEPTEMBER 21

—ᴍ—

How I need to see you working in majesty and might and glory! We all need just that touch of yours making all things new and wonderful, countering any influence or standard other than your own. Purify and empower us with your presence.

APRIL 12

—◦◦◦—

How we need just you!
Make it a day forever
memorable for intimacy
with you.

SEPTEMBER 20

—◦◦◦—

Lord, come and touch all our
lives and the atmosphere of the
college with energizing power
and sweetness.

APRIL 13

—⁓—

O Lord, how reluctant my nature
seems to dwell on the profound
truths of your grace, even though
I know the power and purity of
communion with you.

SEPTEMBER 19

———⚬———

Lord, what manner of man ought I to
be! The graciousness of my life under
your rule is so marvelous, and yet I find
myself so ungenerous and ungracious.
Lord, what shall I say?

APRIL 14

—※—

O Lord, bless us this day.
Save us from indolence and
spiritual sloth, and cause your
initiatives to be almighty.

SEPTEMBER 18

—⋙—

Lord, for the college, permeate
it today with your presence and
salvation from the top room to the
basement. Bless with vigor and
keenness mentally and spiritually.

APRIL 15

—✺—

Lord, I ask to see you. I have been
preoccupied and away from you in my
physical life. Forgive me, and draw me
near to yourself that I may have rare
communion with you again.

SEPTEMBER 17

—◇—

Lord, guide our hearts into your purposes.
So many have come into the glorious but
perilous condition of openness toward you.
Lord, work within us a mighty influx of
your power in correcting and health-giving
fullness of life.

APRIL 16

—◦◦◦—

O Lord, I have a great implicit yearning for a token of your notice. Give just a sign that you are using me for something in your purpose.

SEPTEMBER 16

———

Lord, how I praise you for this
college. It has been four years
of unique loveliness, and now
I give it up because I believe I do
so in answer to your call.

APRIL 17

—⁂—

O Lord my God, my strength, my
hope, and my joy, slowly but surely
I seem to be emerging into a clearer
understanding of you. Dawn through
all earth-born clouds and mists today.

SEPTEMBER 15

—◦◦◦—

Lord, yesterday the YMCA accepted me for their work in the desert camps in Egypt, and your word came this morning with great emphasis—sent "before His face into every city and place where He Himself was about to go" (Luke 10:1).

APRIL 18

—◦—

O Lord, so many to pray
for, so many in need of
deliverance. How hungrily
I look up to you today.

SEPTEMBER 14

—✦—

O Lord, I turn to you, nothing
to perceive but just you. Take
the elaborate and the heroic and
the impulsive, and enable me to
quietly wait on you.

APRIL 19

—— ✺ ——

Lord, put your mouth to our college life and breathe the invigorating breath of your re-creating life through us all, putting sickness far from us.

SEPTEMBER 13

———✎———

How complete must be my hold on you
else through sheer futility I wilt and
wander and am only weak. In my present
mood I am inclined to give way to the
feeling of having missed the mark. Lord,
deal with my mind and outlook.

APRIL 20

—◦—

O Lord, I do rejoice at your word,
"as one who finds great treasure"
(Psalm 119:162). As I speak today
put your words in my mouth. Be so
present that it shall be evident to all
that it is your word.

SEPTEMBER 12

—⚬—

My soul's horizon reports, like
Elijah's servant, "There is nothing"
(1 Kings 18:43). Every door of
opportunity seems closed.
Keep me unhurried.

APRIL 21

O Lord, with the coming of spring in
nature my spirit longs that your energizing
life may flow in and through me more, and
still yet more. But how un-beautiful I am,
how un-Christlike! And yet it is not in
depression, but in amazing hope I see this.

SEPTEMBER 11

—⚬—

Lord, you know the strangeness of the
lull in the opening up of the future;
nothing manifests itself. I have such
a great need just now for exaltation
of mood and mind and manner.
Bring confirmation to my mind.

APRIL 22

———❦———

O Lord, draw me to you; give me
the glorious sensing of yourself
that makes a mere sinner like me
worthy as your servant.

SEPTEMBER 10

—◦—

Lord, as we begin to intercede for our country at our morning prayers, I ask that your Spirit will direct us.

APRIL 23

O Lord, "that Your eyes may be open toward this [house] night and day" (1 Kings 8:29). Keep it and guard it from all that is not in your order, and cause each one of us to be all that your secret heart desires.

SEPTEMBER 9

—⁂—

Lord, a vague desolation seems around my life.
It is nebulous, I cannot define it. I have no misgiving
over my decision for I have done what you indicated
I should do, but still the sense of uncertainty
remains. Touch this nebulous nimbus and turn it
into a horizon of ordered beauty and form.

APRIL 24

———✧———

O Lord, in humbled manner
I pray this morning, full of
adoration and worship, but full
of humility when I remember
how shielded my life is.

SEPTEMBER 8

———✦———

My mind is still vague regarding the way I am to take, Lord. So much has gone beyond my own discernment in this decision. It is not that I doubt you, but all is so completely shrouded.

APRIL 25

—⁓—

O Lord, disentangle me; I have a great
longing for a simplicity of relationship
with you that shall transfigure
everything and shed blessing and
benediction all around.

SEPTEMBER 7

⚊⚬⚊

Lord, I feel myself craving the external sense of your presence, the hundredfold more of your joyous benediction. Lord, I leave this desire with you; grant it as you see best.

APRIL 26

—⚬—

O Lord, restore the keen edge of all
spiritual sensibilities. Lift me into
your light by your abounding grace
through our Lord Jesus Christ.
How slow I am to apprehend more
of you and of your ways!

SEPTEMBER 6

—◆◆◆—

How unsettled my mind has been
about the future. I praise you that this
is not always so, or scarcely ever so.
How there is nothing to hold to but
just yourself! Keep me from flagging
and slacking.

APRIL 27

—⁓—

O Lord, this day I have to speak in your name three times, and I am un-moved and un-inspired till now. If you can convey your mind to me in my spiritual dullness, oh, for Jesus Christ's sake, do it.

SEPTEMBER 5

—⁂—

For the devotional meeting,
make it a time, I pray you,
of the unveiling of your face.
We need just you, and your
ineffable sweetness and beauty.

APRIL 28

—᙭—

O Lord my God, assist me to worship you. I praise you that you remain forever the same. Touch me, O Lord, and by your power renew me spiritually to eagerness and appreciation of you and of your truth.

SEPTEMBER 4

—❦—

Lord, cause your loving-kindness
to be known by me this day by
your inevitably powerful touches,
and use me in your gentle
almightiness for your purposes.

APRIL 29

—◆—

O Lord, dawn on us and draw us into yourself today; begin with me. Cleanse me, O Lord, from all the imperfections which are clear to you though not to me.

SEPTEMBER 3

—∿—

Lord, be to me a place of broad rivers, full of life and restful activity. Show each one of us more love and gentleness today, and to me, because so many are influenced directly by me.

APRIL 30

—⊷—

"The Lord reigns." O Lord, let your reigning power be manifested this day in the bodies of your servants for your glory.

SEPTEMBER 2

❧

O Lord, swamp me with
your grace and glory that
the ample tide of yourself
may be all in all.

MAY 1

—⟨⟩—

Lord, I praise you for this day's glad
opportunity of serving you acceptably.
I bless you for the revealing of the
truth that your order comes moment
by moment in the day's life.

SEPTEMBER 1

———※———

Lord, I have decided before you
to offer to work for the Forces.
Take control and guide me in each
particular. I know you will, but I am
fearful of my own hasty judgment.

MAY 2

—◆—

"But when the kindness and the love of God our Savior toward man appeared . . ." (Titus 3:4)—O Lord, that verse haunts me. How little of your kindness and your love I exhibit toward others!

AUGUST 31

—⋙—

Lord, to you I look, help me to worship
you well. I praise you that my nature
does worship you, but my conscious
life is slow to respond to you and your
beauty as it might. Lord, help me.

MAY 3

—⁓—

May the power and tone and health
of God be all-pervading this day.
How I long for your generous-
heartedness to be realized in and
through all things! Keep the sense of
your call in me fresh and vivid.

AUGUST 30

———⚬———

Bless the whole college with waves of
health and power. Show us more love
that radiantly in your care we may
go forth this day. Bless the strangers
within our gates.

MAY 4

—⁂—

O Lord, I praise you for the throne
of grace, and that in Jesus Christ
I can draw near with boldness to
receive mercy and grace for this day's
glorifying of you.

AUGUST 29

———— ∾ ————

Lord, bring mighty showers of
grace and glory upon all the classes
today, and for the meeting tonight,
I beseech you make it a time of
great power and blessing.

MAY 5

———⟨⟩———

I praise you, O Lord, for your gift of
salvation, for the benefit and blessing
of the prayers of the saints. But how
I slip into your gifts and slowly begin
to think I merit them, or act as though
I did. Forgive me, Lord.

AUGUST 28

—◦◦◦—

Lord, how complete and entire and
absolute is my need of you in every way
and in all ways. I am a vast cavity for
you to fill; fill me to overflowing with
your glory and beauty.

MAY 6

—⁕—

I would, O Lord, cleanse myself
from all defilement of flesh and
spirit, from every coarsening of the
fiber of the spiritual life, so that I
may dwell in you in fullness of joy.

AUGUST 27

—⁂—

Fill the college with your glorious
benediction and blessing.
Go in and out among us today,
charging the atmosphere with
your gracious presence.

MAY 7

---•—

O Lord, I praise you that through
Christ Jesus our Lord it is mercy and
loving-kindness, graciousness and
wonders, all along the way. I desire to be
more sensitive to you and your doings,
more Christlike in my gratitude.

AUGUST 26

—⁓—

Lord, I know that you abound in grace
and are always well; grant me that
grace and well-being. You know how
much our spiritual life depends on our
feeling well physically.

MAY 8

―⁓―

O Lord, by your grace, I see so much with my mind and speak so much—cause my heart and my conduct not only to keep pace with my mind but go far beyond it.

AUGUST 25

———— ❦ ————

Lord, so much truth revealed,
so many things to say, and so little
do I feel I live up to what you
show me. Lord, empower me for
your glory.

MAY 9

—⟶—

O Lord, I thank you for your word,
"'Not by might nor by power, but by
My Spirit,' says the LORD of hosts"
(Zechariah 4:6). I ask for such aid of
your Spirit that you may be satisfied
with me today.

AUGUST 24

—◦◦◦—

Lord, visit us with the manifestation
of your life today. Cause a breath of
emancipation to begin and flow on
unto you, confirming in godliness and
grace each one of us here.

MAY 10

—⦿—

Lord, through all the countless
duties of the day keep me
calm. Uplift me by your touch
and tenderness. Settle and
quiet me in you.

AUGUST 23

—◦◦◦—

Lord, lift me as I lift myself up
to you. Give me the light of
your countenance that I may
shine it back to you.

MAY 11

—⁂—

O Lord, I lift up my eyes, my hopes, and my prayers to you. Reenergize me from your heights by the indwelling of your Holy Spirit that the light of God may arise around and in us today. Fill up the day with sweetness and glory for your own delight.

AUGUST 22

—◦—

Lord, I am writing "The Discipline of Prayer." Fill and inspire me, and cause the little booklet to be all you desire it should be.

MAY 12

O Lord, I pray for more love—
passionate, devout, and earnest love to
you—to show itself in my conscious life.
Oh for grace to show and to feel patience
and gentleness to those around me!

AUGUST 21

—⚬—

Lord, touch me physically that
that well-being of yours may
wash the shores of my life and
fill me with praise.

MAY 13

―――❧―――

O Lord, you are what I am longing for!
"My soul thirsts for God, for the living
God. When shall I come and appear
before God?" (Psalm 42:2). Oh, for
your touch, your life, your beauty; let it
come now, Lord, even as I pray.

AUGUST 20

—※—

Lord, I praise you that you have
prevented my seeking things
immediately for myself, but just your
touch I do seek, a token for good—
but not if it will hinder your
well-being in me.

MAY 14

—◦◦◦—

O Lord, how clearly you have
shown me that it is God,
and God alone, who matters.
May I never stumble any in
this great realization.

AUGUST 19

—⧉—

"If you ask anything in My name, I will do
it" (John 14:14). It is all so mysterious,
O Lord, and all so simple—I pray, and
believe that you do create something in
answer to and by the very means of my
prayer that was not in existence before.

MAY 15

─※─

O Lord, I realize how little of the hidden life of believing in Jesus I have exercised lately; ulterior motives seem to creep in all the time. Bring the simplicity that is in Christ into my life and outlook in deeper ways—careful only of your approval.

AUGUST 18

—⁓—

Lord, with your purity permeate our
minds and bodies and affections;
let us realize and quickly manifest the
enlivening of your ways. Come into
our circumstances in the abundance
of your power.

MAY 16

—⚬—

O Lord, touch all our lives with
your energizing power and loving-
kindness and beauty; make it a
time of the unveiling of your face.
This seems to be all my prayer.

AUGUST 17

—〜〜—

I desire, O Lord, to see your face
and know your power and thrilling
grace. Draw me close to you in full
recuperation, and forgive me for the
neglect of your ways in external details.

MAY 17

—◆—

O Lord this day, cause your glorious
voice to be heard, and heard by me.
Oh speak to me, produce your stillness
in my heart and mind and speak with
thrilling power.

AUGUST 16

—✦—

Lord, have us all completely in
your hand, enabling us to choose
your leading that "our God would
count [us] worthy of this calling"
(2 Thessalonians 1:11).

MAY 18

—⁓—

Lord, this Sabbath morning, insulate
me from distracting sights and sounds.
Loosen me from the bands that bind
me to the present and the recent, and
fill with your Spirit the whole limit of
this day.

AUGUST 15

—⁓—

Lord, I feel myself longing for you
and your life, and I am turning to the
91st Psalm for assurance—"Surely He
shall deliver you" (verse 3). Lord, I am
assured of it. Thank you for the sweet
sense of your protecting care.

MAY 19

—⚬—

"Like rain upon the mown grass" (Psalm 72:6 NASB); "like the dew to Israel" (Hosea 14:5)—O Lord, these phrases come to my mind this morning with sweet insistence. Be as rain and as dew to us this day, refreshing, remolding, and blessing us. To you I come in great and glad expectancy.

AUGUST 14

—⚬⚬⚬—

"Holiness, without which no one will see the Lord" (Hebrews 12:14): Lord, I thank you for that word. How awful if you were not holy! How easy it would seem at times to decline into a lesser, baser life. I thank you for the warning.

MAY 20

—⁓—

O Lord, how complete is my need of
you! To you I come; give me a gracious
renewing of your life till my reasoning
powers, my imagination, and my
speaking are all of you. I seek your
touch and thrilling grace today.

AUGUST 13

—◆—

Lord, gather my powers to yourself,
save from dissipation of energy,
and cure all ailments with your
perfect health. Come and make the
whole limit of this bodily temple shine
with your presence.

MAY 21

—⧓—

Lord, I would like to pour out my heart
before you—my soul is not brilliant in
experience just now, nor my intellect
vigorous, both are jaded; but I adore you
that you are never dull nor jaded, and that
you know our frame (Psalm 103:14).

AUGUST 12

—∾—

How helpless I am in bringing forth
fruit, your kind of fruit in the world,
so ungenerous and unlike you am I.
Forgive me, and by abiding in Jesus
may I bear much fruit and so glorify
the Father.

MAY 22

—⁂—

O Lord, speak to me now.
Inspire me for today—dullness,
deep and devastating, seems to
hold fast to my powers.

AUGUST 11

———

Lord, I praise you for this place I am in,
but the wonder has begun to stir in me—
is this your place for me? Hold me steady
doing your will. It may be only restlessness;
if so, calm me to strength that I do not sin
against you by doubting.

MAY 23

—◦⦙◦—

O Lord, how complete is my
need of you! Come into our
actual circumstances this day in
the abundance of your power.

AUGUST 10

———

With worshipping reverence I draw near to
you this morning in the awareness that you are
my Father, and fully know of the patience you
have had with me in my unreality. But, Lord,
I do not seem to care now if I am real or not
because you yourself are the great Reality.

MAY 24

—~~—

O Lord, how slow I am to show in
my actions the gracious grace of
God! When shall your beauty be
upon me for your honor?

AUGUST 9

───✦───

Lord, how completely I need you
and ache for you. Return unto me
in completeness, and as your life fills
up the limits of mind and spirit and
overflows, glory will be to your name.

MAY 25

———— ❧ ————

Lord God Omnipotent, how my soul
delights to know that you care for
sparrows and number the hairs of
our head! Lord, breathe on me till
I am in the frame of mind and body
to worship you.

AUGUST 8

—⊶⊷—

Lord, bring your light and grace
to bear upon us. May we "adorn
the doctrine of God our Savior
in all things" (Titus 2:10).

MAY 26

~᭥~

O Lord, rise in grandeur into our
lives and ways and goings. Be a
strong presence of healing and
hope and grace and beauty this day.

AUGUST 7

—⌗—

Lord, extricating and beautifying are the
two things my soul most needs today.
To you I come as an incarnate need of you
as Savior and Lord. Repair all the loss of
spiritual bloom and sensitivity to you that
I may be the right influence for you here.

MAY 27

—✦—

Breathe on me, breath of God,
until my mind and spirit are in
suitable adjustment to yourself.
Pour out liberty and purity and
power among and in us all.

AUGUST 6

—✶—

Lord, I adore you for the past college
term. How many you have allowed
me to see enter gloriously into a right
relationship with you! It is too wonderful
for me to praise you adequately.

MAY 28

—⚬—

O Lord, how all things are
simple and glorious when you
are seen! This day let me see
your face and be alone with you.

AUGUST 5

—◆—

O Lord, my God, how wonderfully
and powerfully you have caused me
to know with a knowledge that passes
knowledge that redemption is the one
great revelation reality.

MAY 29

―※―

O Lord, make this a right royal day
with you. Touch us, O Lord, that all
our spiritual and material life may be
attuned to your purposes. Just your
touch, and all will be well.

AUGUST 4

—⁂—

Lord, how similar I am to the man who had
nothing to set before the friend who came
to him at midnight (Luke 11:5–6)! So many
are in need of emancipation and deliverance,
undertake completely. Sweep through the
whole college with your gracious presence.

MAY 30

—∞—

"Whoever is wise . . . will understand the lovingkindness of the LORD" (Psalm 107:43). Lord, that would be beautiful! Give me this token for your glory. I look to you for this day; cause the abundance of your bounty and beauty to be upon us.

AUGUST 3

———

Lord, this day I have to preach in
your name; make it radiant with
your power. Draw out my soul into
the great realization of yourself,
keep me centralized in you in every
deep and final sense.

MAY 31

O Lord, how essentially
necessary it is for me to
draw near to you. How can I
falter when you are my life?

AUGUST 2

—✺—

Lord, call me by name that I may thrill
with that wonderful calling! What
a difference a little thing for you to
do does make—a calling by name, a
passing touch, and we are in ecstasy!
Oh, why do you not do it more often?

JUNE 1

———⚬———

O Lord, how I realize my need
of a worthier conception of you.
All lesser things I would merge
into this petition—that I might
worthily magnify you.

AUGUST 1

—⁓—

"My spirit's weather"—how aptly that describes my condition today! Control it, and help me to rise in it and above it.

———

Quotation from *The Diary of an Old Soul* by George MacDonald.

JUNE 2

—⁓—

"Light is sown for the righteous" (Psalm 97:11). Lord, what a harvest! How wonderful are your ways.

JULY 31

—◆◆◆—

O Lord, my soul lives before you
in adoration for your mighty grace
bestowed on me, so that my eyes
see and my ears hear and my heart
understands your presence and actions
behind all circumstances.

JUNE 3

———❦———

O Lord, I marvel at my slowness in
praise; enliven me to praise you.
Give me a powerful realization of your
goodness, that I might be a joyous
satisfaction to your own heart.

JULY 30

—◆—

This morning, O Lord, I praise
you for all the past—so wayward
on my part, so gracious and
long-suffering and forgiving and
tender on yours.

JUNE 4

—◦◦◦—

Lord, in complete
dependence I look to you;
it is good for me to feel
"wandered" till you appear.

JULY 29

—◦◦◦—

Lord, the range of your power, the
touch of your grace, the breathing
of your Spirit—how I long for these
to bring me face-to-face with you.
Forgive my tardiness—it takes me so
long to awaken to some things.

JUNE 5

—⚬—

"In this you greatly rejoice, though now for a little while, if need be, you have been grieved by various trials" (1 Peter 1:6). O Lord, I rejoice that the "if need be" is yours! And I praise you for the counsel to "not think it strange concerning the fiery trial" (1 Peter 4:12) but to rejoice.

JULY 28

—⚬⚬⚬—

O Lord, save us from the
murmuring spirit that for the
majority of us is merely skin-deep,
but is harmful, hurting the bloom
of spiritual communion.

JUNE 6

O Lord, I pray for the power of your Spirit to adore you in fuller ways. Keep my spirit brightly infused by your Holy Spirit that thus energized, the Lord Jesus and His perfections may be manifested in my mortal flesh.

JULY 27

———〰———

Detach me, O Lord, from the things of sense and time, and usher me into the presence of the King. Keep the precincts of my mind and heart entirely yours.

JUNE 7

〰️

O Lord, with what abundant relief I turn to you. I need you in unfathomable ways, and with what amazed relief and joy I find all I need is you.

JULY 26

—◦◦◦—

O God, my Father, the clouds are but
the dust of your feet (Nahum 1:3)!
Let me discover in every cloud of
Providence or Nature or Grace no man
except Jesus only after the fear,
till there be no fear.

JUNE 8

O Lord, this morning
disperse every mist, and
shine forth clear and
strong and invigoratingly.

JULY 25

—⦿—

O Lord, I would seek your face,
but what good is my seeking if
you do not reveal yourself?
Show me your face, O Lord.
Keep me ever seeing you.

JUNE 9

—⚬—

You have "enlarged me when I was in distress" (Psalm 4:1 KJV): Oh that the thoughts of my heart were more and more a well-spring of gracious treasure without ceasing!

JULY 24

—◆—

To you, O Lord, I come, may your
beauty and grace and soothing peace be
in and upon me this day, and may no
wind or weather or anxiety ever touch
your peace in my life or in this place.

JUNE 10

—✺—

Lord, your goodness is so beyond comparison that we are "like those who dream," our mouth is "filled with laughter, and our tongue with singing" (Psalm 126:1–2). We praise you for the time when we shall come again with joy, bringing our "sheaves" with us (Psalm 126:6).

JULY 23

—~∞~—

O Lord, I pray for greater sweetness
and beauty of character, for the gift
of spiritual energy and great patience
toward others. Your sweetness, your
beauty, manifest them, O Lord; filled
with you I would be indeed.

JUNE 11

—⚬—

O Lord, draw near, press into
my understanding until I am all
taken up with you. Make this
day radiant with your power.

JULY 22

———— ∞ ————

Lord, bless the devotional meeting today. May it break with soft beauty and sure blessing and special bounty upon us all.

JUNE 12

—⟫⟫⟫—

O Lord, there is no time with you, for "a thousand years in Your sight are like yesterday when it is past" (Psalm 90:4); but with me it is necessarily different. How you have restored the years the locust has eaten (Joel 2:25) and created me a new creature in Christ Jesus! Accept my thanksgiving.

JULY 21

⸻※⸻

O Lord, as we consider the fifty-third chapter of Isaiah this morning, light it up with your glory. Soften and subdue, inspire and thrill, and raise us on to the level of such glorious service that we may catch your likeness.

JUNE 13

—⁓—

O Lord, in might and
majesty prevail in many more
ways today. Keep me from
secularization of soul or spirit.

JULY 20

—◆◆◆—

O Lord, that I might be brought into
your presence, and see things from your
standpoint. I have to speak to your
people this morning; anoint me afresh,
O Lord, with your gracious Spirit.

JUNE 14

—⁂—

O Lord, I know your blessing and I
praise you, but it is the indescribable
touch and encircling, as your servant,
that I seek—I know not what I seek,
but you know. How I long for you!

JULY 19

—⁓—

Cause it to be light and sweetness
and joy all day. Take charge with
your easy power and might.
Graciously dawn on us physically
and mentally and spiritually.

JUNE 15

—m—

O Lord, this day lead me into
some more of your gracious
and wondrous doings. Put your
loving hand of grace and power
upon me this day.

JULY 18

—◇◇◇—

O Lord, I praise you that you are,
and that by your divine omnipotent
grace I am learning to come into your
presence. Touch my body and spirit
with your grace and light and wisdom;
bright and vivid make your touches.

JUNE 16

O Lord, give me the disposition
of mind that delights in you.
Cleanse me from all fog and
flurry and fuss, that clear-eyed I
may see your way this day.

JULY 17

—⚬—

"Unite my heart to fear Your name"
(Psalm 86:11). My soul is wandering and
unfocused because of the ordinariness, the
self-consciousness, the less-than-the-best,
which hover around and prevent me as I pray.
Lord, be almighty for me!

JUNE 17

———

O Lord, I thank you for the
relief and inspiration, the radiant
joy that has flowed into me and
visited my inner kingdom. Fill me
now with your calm peace.

JULY 16

—◆◆◆—

Lord, touch with energizing
power and sweet loving-kindness
and beauty all our lives today;
make it a time of the unveiling
of your face and power.

JUNE 18

—❈—

O Lord, grant that this day may
end forever the self-consciousness
that weakens us in your service, and
may we be conscious only of Jesus.

JULY 15

—⚬—

O Lord, I thank you for the nameless
forebodings and shadows of the mind which
hover around when insufficient time is being
given to prayer. Lord, I look up to you now.
Descend, O gracious Lord, descend, and give
me grace to rejoice in you this day.

JUNE 19

―――⚬―――

O Lord, how I long for you
to bring me face-to-face with
yourself! My soul thirsts for you,
for the touch of your grace, the
breathing of your Spirit.

JULY 14

—⦿—

Lord, that I might see you, feel you, "faith" you, and fully realize you in the manner and measure you see I am capable of. What do I wait for but for you only?

JUNE 20

⸺

O Lord, anoint the college to
praise you. Bring the buoyant
breezes of your Holy Spirit
upon us now.

JULY 13

—◦〰◦—

Oh, by your indwelling Spirit knit
me together into worship and
beauty and holiness. Lord, touch
my body and spirit till both are
sweeping in one for you.

JUNE 21

———✦———

O Lord, rouse and quicken
me so that I may indeed be
the obedient, docile servant
of your Spirit.

JULY 12

—⁓—

Touch my spirit till it be filled
with you to overflowing.
Think through my mind till I form
the mind "which was also in Christ
Jesus" (Philippians 2:5).

JUNE 22

—◦◦◦—

Lord, what an intense need of you I realize this morning. Supply that need according to your riches in Christ Jesus until I am wholly transfigured by the supply.

JULY 11

—⁓—

Send us more students, O Lord,
until this place is filled with
men and women through
whom you can glorify yourself
throughout the world.

JUNE 23

—⚬—

O Lord, draw your powerful
presence around me this
day as a curtain, and be the
glory in the midst.

JULY 10

—⚬⚬⚬—

Bless us all this day, guard minds
and hearts from vague fancies
and false emotions, from shadows
of the imagination, and keep us
wholesomely yours.

JUNE 24

—◦◦◦—

O Lord, remove this bondage
of thought, and bring peace and
purity and power. Fill me this
day with your tenderness and
compassion and grace.

JULY 9

—◆◆◆—

O Lord, how much the margins
of my mind are taken up with
surrounding interests of late so that
the surroundings seem the center.
Be my strong Center and Surrounding.

JUNE 25

---✦---

O Lord, breathe on me till I am one
with you in the attitude of my mind
and heart and disposition. To you
I turn. How completely I realize my
lost-ness without you!

JULY 8

O Lord, what great and glorious outlines
have passed and are passing before the vision
of our personal spirits about your plans.
Lord, we do not see the way, but we know
you and trust. Keep our minds and hearts
strong and quiet in you.

JUNE 26

—◦—

O Lord, to praise you properly
is a great desire of mine,
created and fostered by your
Spirit and grace.

JULY 7

———

"I was so foolish and ignorant; I was like a beast before You" (Psalm 73:22). O Lord, those words express me to myself before you. I am ashamed of my attitude, so foolish, so "beast-ly," when looked at in the light of the pure and holy God-likeness our Lord demands.

JUNE 27

—✦—

Lord, so much activity, so
many things, so numberless
the people! Bless today with
largeness of heart and beauty
of character for your glory.

JULY 6

O Lord, to you I come with praise and thanksgiving, but with a yearning for a deeper conscious appreciation of your goodness. Bless me this day with an enlarged capacity and power to praise.

JUNE 28

———⧸⧹———

Lord, I would bless and praise you, but
how hard I find it to praise you when I am
not physically fit. Yet why should it be so?
This means that I praise you only when
it is a pleasure to me. I desire that my soul
were one continual praise to you!

JULY 5

—◦◦◦—

Lord, I bless you for this college, that
in it you are proving "a strength to the
poor, a strength to the needy in his
distress, a refuge from the storm, a
shade from the heat" (Isaiah 25:4).

JUNE 29

———ᴥ———

O Lord, lift up the light of your
countenance upon us this day and
make us fit in with your plans with
great sweetness and liberty, and a
buoyant spirit toward you all day.

JULY 4

—◆◆◆—

Lord, my mind is dim in relation to _____.
Lord, be their strong tower; none seem to
regard them or care. Prevent the enemy
from squeezing them. They are as they
are because of their loyalty to you.
Lord, undertake mightily.

JUNE 30

—◦—

Lord, how I desire to see you, to hear you, to meditate on you, and to visibly grow more like you! And you have said, "Delight yourself also in the LORD, and He shall give you the desires of your heart" (Psalm 37:4).

JULY 3

—⁂—

O Lord, bless this day. These students,
O Lord, into your hands I commend them.
You know it is with a clear definite plan of my
own I meet them day by day, but I thank you
that you have your own great plans. Carry
them out, O Lord, with power and grace.

JULY 1

—⚬—

"Casting all your care upon Him, for He cares for you" (1 Peter 5:7). O Lord, what a wonder these words are! The toxic atmosphere that at times lies around the margins of the mind needs your constant care to keep it away. I look to you that I may be renewed in the spirit of my mind.

JULY 2

—⚬—

Keep this college, O Lord, spiritually
and in all ways, "exceedingly
magnificent" (1 Chronicles 22:5).
Give us the light and illumination
you delight in.